A Crabtree Roots Book

Collection Crabtree « Les racines »

DELIVERY PERSON
LES LIVREURS

People I Meet

Les gens que je rencontre

DOUGLAS BENDER

Crabtree Publishing

crabtreebooks.com

School-to-Home Support for Caregivers and Teachers

This book helps children grow by letting them practice reading. Here are a few guiding questions to help the reader with building his or her comprehension skills. Possible answers appear here in red.

Before Reading:

- What do I think this book is about?
    - *This book is about delivery people.*
    - *This book is about what a delivery person does at work.*
- What do I want to learn about this topic?
    - *I want to learn what a delivery person looks like.*
    - *I want to learn what a delivery person does.*

During Reading:

- I wonder why...
    - *I wonder why some people become delivery people.*
    - *I wonder why delivery people wear uniforms.*
- What have I learned so far?
    - *I have learned that some delivery people drive trucks.*
    - *I have learned that delivery people help deliver packages.*

After Reading:

- What details did I learn about this topic?
    - *I have learned that delivery people wear uniforms.*
    - *I have learned that delivery people have to be strong to carry a lot of packages.*
- Read the book again and look for the vocabulary words.
    - *I see the word* ***scanner*** *on page 6 and the word* ***uniform*** *on page 8. The other vocabulary words are found on page 14.*

Soutien de l’école à la maison pour les gardien(ne)s et les enseignant(e)s.

Ce livre aide les enfants à se développer grâce à la pratique de la lecture. Voici quelques exemples de questions pour aider le lecteur ou la lectrice à développer ses capacités de compréhension. Les suggestions de réponses sont indiquées en rouge.

Avant la lecture

- De quoi ce livre parle-t-il?
    - *Ce livre parle des livreurs.*
    - *Ce livre parle de ce que fait un livreur au travail.*
- Qu’est-ce que je veux apprendre sur ce sujet
    - *Je veux apprendre à quoi ressemble un livreur.*
    - *Je veux apprendre ce que fait un livreur.*

Pendant la lecture

- Je me demande pourquoi...
    - *Je me demande pourquoi certaines personnes deviennent des livreurs.*
    - *Je me demande pourquoi les livreurs portent un uniforme.*
- Qu’est-ce que j’ai appris jusqu’à présent?
    - *J’ai appris que certains livreurs conduisent une camionnette.*
    - *J’ai appris que les livreurs aident à livrer les paquets.*

Après la lecture

- Nomme quelques détails que tu as retenus
    - *J’ai appris que les livreurs portent un uniforme.*
    - *J’ai appris que les livreurs doivent être forts pour porter beaucoup de paquets.*
- Lis le livre à nouveau et cherche les mots de vocabulaire.
    - *Je vois le mot* ***scanneur*** *à la page 6 et le mot* ***uniforme*** *à la page 8. Les autres mots de vocabulaire se trouvent à la page 14.*

This is a **delivery person**.

Voici un **livreur**.

A delivery person delivers **packages**.

La livreuse livre des **paquets**.

A delivery person has a **scanner**.

Le livreur a un **scanneur**.

A delivery person has a **uniform**.

Le livreur porte un **uniforme**.

Some delivery people have a **van**.

Certains livreurs ont une **camionnette**.

Do you know a delivery person?

Connais-tu un livreur ou une livreuse?

Word List

Sight Words

a	some
do	this
has	you
is	

Liste de mots

Mots courants

a	tu
certains	un
la	une
le	

Words to Know

delivery person

packages

scanner

uniform

van

La boîte à mots

camionnette

livreur

paquets

scanneur

uniforme

34 Words

This is a **delivery person**.
A delivery person delivers **packages**.
A delivery person has a **scanner**.
A delivery person has a **uniform**.
Some delivery people have a **van**.
Do you know a delivery person?

29 mots

Voici un **livreur**.
La livreuse livre des **paquets**.
Le livreur a un **scanneur**.
Le livreur porte un **uniforme**.
Certains livreurs ont une **camionnette**.
Connais-tu un livreur ou une livreuse?

People I Meet

Les gens que je rencontre

DELIVERY PERSON

LES LIVREURS

Written by/Auteur: Douglas Bender
Designed by/Conception: Rhea Wallace
Series development/Développement des séries: James Earley
Proofreader/Relectrice: Janine Deschenes
Educational consultant/Conseillère pédagogique: Marie Lemke M.Ed.
Translated by/Traduction: Jean-Pierre Gaston

Photographs/Références photographiques: Shutterstock: AlexS: cover; Monkey Business Images: p. 1; MichaelJung: p. 3, 14; Drazen Zigic: p. 5, 14; Rido: p. 7, 14; puhha: p. 9, 13, 14; Gorodenkeff: p. 10, 14

La forme masculine est utlilisée dans cet ouvrage uniquement dans le but d'en alléger la forme et d'en faciliter la lecture.

Crabtree Publishing

crabtreebooks.com 800-387-7650

Published in Canada
Publié au Canada
Crabtree Publishing
616 Welland Ave.
St. Catharines, Ontario
L2M 5V6

Published in the United Sta
Publié aux États-Unis
Crabtree Publishing
347 Fifth Avenue,
Suite 1402-145
New York, NY, 10016

Paperback 978-1-0398-5077-4
Ebook (pdf) 978-1-0398-5119-1
Epub 978-1-0398-5161-0

Printed in Canada/122023/CP20231124

Library and Archives Canada Cataloguing in Publication
Available at the Library and Archives Canada

Library of Congress Cataloging-in-Publication Data
Available at the Library of Congress